TITLES & PRICES	DWY	ATOS	GRL	LXL	ISBN
Each Book: $27.07 List / **$18.95 Library**					
Complete Set (8 books): $216.56 List / **$151.60 Library** SAVE $64.96!					
Biking, Arnold Ringstad ©2015					978-16314-34495
Camping, M. J. York ©2015	796	TBD	TBD	550L	978-16268-73261
Canoeing, M. J. York ©2015	796	TBD	TBD	610L	978-16268-73278
Fishing, Arnold Ringstad ©2015	796	TBD	TBD	630L	978-16268-73285
Hiking, M. J. York ©2015	796	TBD	TBD	670L	978-16268-73292
Hunting, Arnold Ringstad ©2015	796	TBD	TBD	630L	978-16268-73308
Kayaking, Arnold Ringstad ©2015	796	TBD	TBD	660L	978-16268-73315
Rock Climbing, M. J. York ©2015	796	TBD	TBD	660L	978-16268-73322
	796	TBD	TBD	620L	978-16268-73339

Fishing

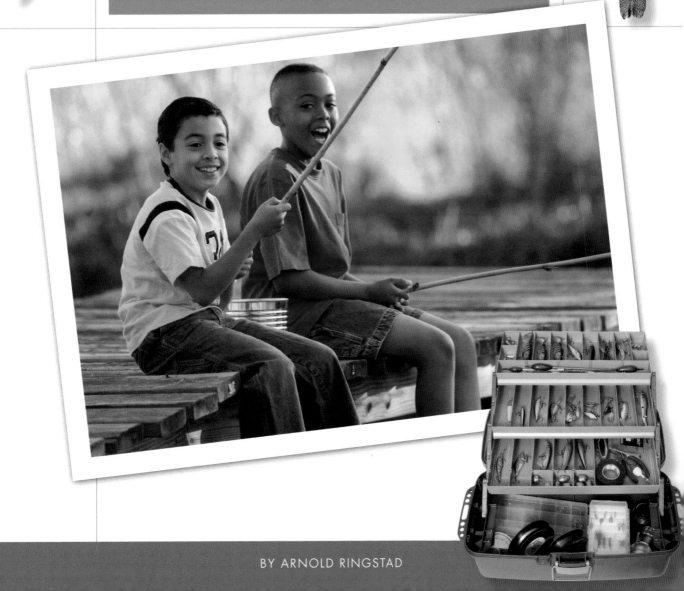

BY ARNOLD RINGSTAD

Published by The Child's World®
1980 Lookout Drive • Mankato, MN 56003-1705
800-599-READ • www.childsworld.com

Acknowledgments
The Child's World®: Mary Berendes, Publishing Director
Red Line Editorial: Editorial direction
The Design Lab: Design
Amnet: Production

Photographs ©: Purestock/Thinkstock, cover (center), 20;
FoodIcons, back cover (top left), 3; Kateryna Dyellalova/
Shutterstock Images, cover (bottom right), 10;
ChicagoStockPhotography/Shutterstock Images, back cover
(bottom), 21; BrandX Images, cover (top left), cover (top right),
back cover (right), 8; Thinkstock, 4–5, 7, 9, 18; Robert Hardin/
Thinkstock, 11; DigitalVision, 12; Comstock Images/Thinkstock,
14; Shutterstock Images, 15; Aleks Key/Shutterstock Images, 16;
iStockphoto, 17; Michael Olson/Thinkstock, 19

ISBN 9781626873292
LCCN 2014930666

Printed in the United States of America
Mankato, MN
July, 2014
PA02222

ABOUT THE AUTHOR

Arnold Ringstad lives in Minnesota. He thinks walleye are the tastiest fish.

CONTENTS

FUN WITH FISHING

Have you ever gone fishing? You can fish almost anywhere there is water. People fish in rushing rivers. Some go fishing in calm lakes. Others fish in the ocean!

People fish for different reasons. Some people do it to eat. Others do it just for fun. They catch fish and release fish back into the water.

Some people enter fishing contests. They compete to catch the biggest fish.

WHAT IS FISHING?

Fishing is the activity of catching fish from the water. People have fished for thousands of years. Originally, they fished to survive. They ate the fish they caught. Today, many people fish for fun and relaxation. They compete to catch large or rare fish. People who fish are also known as **anglers**.

Scientists discovered that people have been eating fish for more than 40,000 years. Early fishermen used nets made of grass. They made hooks out of bone. **Ancient** art in Egypt shows people using fishing rods. Writing from ancient China describes fishing lines and rods.

Anglers fish for fun, relaxation, and competition.

RODS, REELS, AND LINES

Fishing gear is called **tackle**. One of the most important pieces of tackle is the fishing rod. It is a long, thin pole. Rods are usually 5 to 8.5 feet (1.5 to 2.6 m) long. They are made of **fiberglass** or **graphite**. They must be flexible enough to bend when the angler is casting. Casting is throwing a fishing line. Rods also must be strong. This is so fish will not break them.

Another piece of tackle is fishing line. Fishing line is a long, thin strand of material. It is often made of

Fishing rods are long and flexible.

nylon. The strength of a line is measured in test strength. The test strength usually ranges from 2 to 25 pounds (0.9 to 11.3 kg). Bigger fish require line with higher test strength.

Fishing line works with the rod and a piece of tackle called a reel. Together, they make fishing possible. The reel is connected to the rod near the rod's base. Fishing line is wound around the center of the reel. One end of the line exits the reel and travels up the rod. The reel has a handle on the outside. This lets the angler pull the fish in once it bites.

ANCIENT GEAR
Ancient people did not have fiberglass, graphite, and nylon for their tackle. They had to use the materials around them. For example, in ancient China, anglers used rods made of bamboo.

Fishing reels hold fishing line.

IN THE TACKLE BOX

Anglers store important tackle in a tackle box. An organized tackle box makes it easy to find the tackle you need to catch the fish you want. Anglers often keep hooks, lures, and floats in their tackle boxes.

Fishhooks are tied to the end of the line. Fishhooks are sharp, curved pieces of metal. An angler pushes the hook through **bait** to keep the bait in place. Bait can be a live animal, such as a worm or insect. This kind of bait is called natural bait. Fish try to eat the animal. Their mouths get stuck on the hook.

Anglers keep their gear in a tackle box.

Fishing lures are bait that is not alive. Lures often are made of plastic or metal. Some are shaped like fish or insects. Others are shiny to attract the fish. One or more hooks may be attached to a lure.

Another piece of tackle is called a float or bobber. It is connected to the line a short distance above the bait. The float stays on the surface of the water. It helps anglers know a fish has taken the bait below the surface. When a fish bites on the bait, the fish starts to swim away. When it does, the float sinks under the surface. Then, the angler knows to reel in the fish.

Floats help anglers know if they have a fish on the line.

PLACES TO FISH

Fish can live in nearly any body of water. Some are in tiny ponds. Others live in the oceans. Some fish swim in calm lakes. Others live in rushing rivers.

Different kinds of fish live in different bodies of water.

However, people cannot go fishing wherever they want. Usually, anglers need a fishing **license**. The license allows them to catch certain kinds of fish in certain areas. Fishing without a license is often illegal. Fishing laws vary from state to state. Different countries have different laws. Anglers must pay to get a fishing license. Governments use the money to protect **endangered** fish. It is used to educate people about fishing. It helps governments create maps of lakes and rivers.

ICE FISHING
Frozen lakes do not stop people from fishing. Anglers who live in cold places go fishing on icy lakes. They drill a hole in the ice about 5 inches (12 cm) wide. They use a short, light rod called a jigging rod. Anglers use bait to attract fish under the ice.

FRESHWATER FISHING

Freshwater is water that is not salty. Water in lakes, rivers, and streams is usually freshwater. Fishing on these waters is called freshwater fishing. Anglers fish from shore, docks, or small boats. They also fish from bridges over rivers. Many kinds of fish live in freshwater. Some of the most common are bass, trout, walleye, and catfish.

Anglers on the shore often use bait or spin casting. They put bait at the end of the line. They flick the rod to

Freshwater ponds, lakes, and rivers are good places to fish.

launch the line into the water. When anglers feel a fish bite, they reel in the line. Some anglers go fly-fishing. Fly-fishing anglers do not use bait. Instead, they use lures called flies. The flies are very light. Anglers need special equipment to use them. They use fly rods and fly reels. Anglers fly-fish from the banks of ponds or rivers. Sometimes, they even stand in the water while they fish.

Anglers on boats often use trolling. In trolling, they cast their bait into the water. Then they move the boat slowly across the lake. The bait is dragged through the water. If a fish bites, anglers pull it into the boat.

CATCH AND RELEASE

If you are fishing for fun, release your fish back into the water. This is called catch and release fishing. This method helps make sure there are enough fish for anglers to catch.

Trout is a common freshwater fish.

SALTWATER FISHING

Ocean water is salty. Fishing in the ocean is called **saltwater** fishing. Saltwater anglers fish from beaches or boats. Bluefish, tarpon,

Saltwater fishing is an exciting activity.

and bonefish are common fish anglers catch from the shore. Anglers on boats often catch flounder, snapper, and mackerel.

One special type of fishing is done on the ocean. It is called big-game fishing. Anglers use motorized boats to chase large fish. They use huge fishing rods with very tough lines. Anglers strap themselves into chairs. They attach their rods to the chairs. They try to catch huge fish, such as tuna, swordfish, and sharks. These fish can weigh hundreds of pounds.

GIGANTIC FISH

Big-game anglers catch some of the biggest fish in the world. The record for the largest fish caught was set in 1959 in Australia. An angler caught a great white shark weighing 2,664 pounds (1,208 kg)!

Great white sharks are very large fish.

FISHING SAFETY

Fishing is usually not a dangerous activity. There are many things anglers can do to stay safe. Always wear a life jacket when fishing from a boat. If you fall off the boat, it could save your life. Fishing with friends is always a good idea. They can rescue you if you fall into the water.

Anglers should also wear proper clothing. Some pieces of tackle, such as hooks, are very sharp. Wear shoes in case you accidentally step on them. Anglers should watch their surroundings when casting. They don't want to throw their hooks over a power line or into a person.

Always wear a life jacket when you fish from a boat.

ICE FISHING SAFETY

Ice fishing can be dangerous. If the ice is not thick enough, it could crack without warning. Falling into icy water can be deadly. Always ask an expert to see whether the ice is thick enough to support your weight.

Ice fishing is a fun but chilly activity.

ENJOYING THE OUTDOORS

There are many ways to have fun with fishing. If you are camping, you might want to fish to catch your dinner. If you want to have fun with

Fishing can be more fun with friends.

friends, you can compete to see who can catch the biggest fish. If you are a talented angler, you can enter public fishing contests.

Relax by spending an afternoon at a lake or river fishing with friends. Fishing is easy for beginners to learn. Yet, it can take a lifetime to become an expert angler. Catch a small trout in a stream or battle a huge swordfish on the ocean. Either way, fishing helps you enjoy the great outdoors.

GLOSSARY

ancient (AYN-chunt): If something is ancient, it is very old. Ancient art in Egypt showed people fishing.

anglers (AN-glurz): Anglers are people who go fishing. People have been anglers for thousands of years.

bait (bayt): Bait is something used to attract fish. Anglers put bait on their fishing lines.

endangered (en-DAYN-jurd): An animal that is endangered is at risk of dying off. Some kinds of fish are endangered.

fiberglass (FYE-bur-glass): Fiberglass is a material made of plastic and glass. Many fishing rods are made of fiberglass.

freshwater (FRESH-wah-dur): Freshwater is water that is not salty. Rivers and lakes often contain freshwater.

graphite (GRA-fiyt): Graphite is a material made out of an element called carbon. Some fishing rods are made of graphite.

license (LYE-sens): A license is a piece of paper that shows someone is allowed to do something. Many states require an angler to buy a fishing license.

nylon (NYE-lawn): Nylon is a synthetic fiber containing plastic. Many fishing lines are made of nylon.

saltwater (SALT-wah-dur): Saltwater is water that is salty. Oceans contain saltwater.

tackle (TACK-ul): Tackle is an angler's fishing gear. Hooks, lures, and fishing line are all pieces of tackle.

TO LEARN MORE

BOOKS

Maas, Dave. *Kids Gone Fishin': The Young Angler's Guide to Catching More and Bigger Fish*. Minnetonka, MN: Creative Publishing International, 2001.

Parker, Steve. *DK Eyewitness Books: Fish*. New York: DK Publishing, 2005.

Seeberg, Tim. *Freshwater Fishing*. North Mankato, MN: The Child's World, 2004.

WEB SITES

Visit our Web site for links about fishing:
childsworld.com/links

Note to Parents, Teachers, and Librarians: We routinely verify our Web links to make sure they are safe and active sites. So encourage your readers to check them out!

INDEX